I0151063

SHARING
REAL LIFE

A COLLECTION OF
STORIES TO INSPIRE
AND ENLIGHTEN

GWENDOLYN JACKSON

NFB
Buffalo, New York

Copyright © 2017 by Gwendolyn Jackson

All rights reserved. No part of this book may be replicated or transmitted on any form or by any means, electronic or mechanical; including photocopying without permission in writing from the Author.

Printed in The United States of America

ISBN: 978-0-9984018-6-7

Sharing Real Life: A Collection of Stories to Inspire and Enlighten/

Jackson-1st ed/

Jackson-1st ed.

1. Christian. 2. Self-Help. 3. Fiction.

4. Short Stories. 5. Jackson.

This is a work of predominantly nonfiction. Some events have been changes in the interest of plot and some of the names have been changed in order to protect privacy.

Unless otherwise indicated, all scriptural quotations are from the King James Version (KJV) of the Bible.

NFB/Amelia Press
<<<>>>
119 Dorchester Road
Buffalo, New York 14213 USA
For more information please visit
nfbpublishing.com

To the One
Who has made all things possible
and inspires the heart to live in victory

Jesus Christ

———————————————

To my family, coworkers, dreamers, imaginers, risk takers, and to life in general for encouraging me to continue using the gifts and talents that were instilled in me from a time before my time existed.

———————————————

Special thanks to Leah Daniel for all her help with the editing process.

Contents

Introduction

Hope To Life   11

The Gas Cap   17

Closed Door   21

Heartstrings   25

Seven Times A Wife   33

After All He Has Done   49

Emancipation Road   53

Home Is Where The Heart Is   57

If You Will Wait   63

My Mr. Mister Story   69

Obedience Is Better   73

Times Three   81

Who Is In The Box?   85

Misery Loves Misery   91

Process It   95

Between A Rock And A Hard Place   97

Idle—Mind Body Soul   103

Truth Be Told   109

Perceptions   117

INTRODUCTION

Some amazing things have happened since the writing of my first book "And It Is So/ Words To Live By" and one of them is the fact that I have never stopped writing. It has now become my life and of course my passion. I am a legitimate writer and I love it. With this being said my second attempt at writing this book should be a little easier but it's not. The flow is still there and the Lord is still inspiring me to tell my experiences but it's a little different this time. The expectation I have of speaking what I think needs to be said has been challenging to say the least and it has put a strain on my creativity. Yet, I do want the book to be the best that it can be because the underlying fabric is to lift Jesus higher so people come to see the magnificence that is He, even if it is one household at a time. My faith is the belief that all my books will inspire not only one person but also their whole household to know who Jesus is in reality and who He is to them personally.

Reaching in to reach out is the basis of ministry, realizing that messages always come to the messenger first to make certain they are the initial partakers of the lessons learned. This means that much of what I write has been tried, tested, and proven profitable to the edifying of the individual soul. Will I tell you everything about my life and let you into the innermost chambers of my mind and heart? No, but I will tell whatever the Lord deems important for those who need to hear that they are not alone. I am someone who is not only sympathetic to their plight but also has empathy, not to judge but to show the same love our Savoir shows us every day. I have been instructed to be real when dealing with His people which may show a little vulnerability on my part but in weakness I can be made strong and so can you   Life is not always good, but what is life without a struggle to make it interesting? My challenge is that you find yourself within each line and the pages that make up this life's story and I know you will.

Practice makes perfect meaning the more talent that is used, subjects are studied, or gifts that are unwrapped, the more enhanced it becomes. Life has a way of showing up in the middle of living. The more life moments accomplished the better because it helps increase faith and a refine trust in God   I am writing my destiny, living in the present seeing the future unfold before my eyes. What a magnificent sight to see!

Hope to Life

Hope is desire accompanied by expectation of fulfillment. It is something hoped for and one that gives promise for the future. Life is vital, vivid, growth and reactive to stimuli. A definition of life is a period during which something continues to function or begins to be interesting, lively, or exciting. To GET A LIFE means to do some thing to improve your situation or to change your lifestyle for the better. It's all good.

A few clichés come to mind when I think of the word hope. One is "keep hope alive", another is "where there is hope there is life." I love the story concerning Abraham and Sarah and the dead seed within both of them. Well into their old age, it really was naturally impossible for them to have a child. However, God's promise is His promise so no matter if you think it can't happen or whatever you believe won't happen it has to be. *Romans 4:18 who against hope believed in hope, that he might become the father of many nations, according to that which was spoken, so shall thy seed be.* He knew it would be against all the odds for Sarah to conceive and no way for him to father another child. God's word was out there that he would be the father of many nations. No artificial insemination or surrogate mother this time around for the promise must be. It is hard to imagine life in this kind of situation but life means growth reactive to stimuli and that stimulus is the Almighty God. And the child was.

Ezekiel had another dilemma to cope with which was to speak life into bones that had been dry for a long time to live again. Life was so nonexistence that was ancient history. This represented God's chosen people who again were following other gods and living sinful lifestyles. The Lord had promised to restore Israel to their rightful place in Him. He said He would forgive their backsliding, punish their enemies, and make them a righteous nation onto Him. Hope is believing something to happen, a vision of a potential event but the Israelites could only see their present circumstances. Even Ezekiel could not see life in what he had to do, yet he had to believe beyond hope. Here he was in the valley of dead situations having a dialogue with the impossible and God asked the question can these bones live? What happened next was more than he would have ever imagined. Bones connected, flesh appeared, breathe was being inhaled and exhaled and life was lived again. There is another chance to get things right.

I would be amiss if I didn't take this opportunity to give my own personal testimony of hope that lead to the life of a dream. Our dream was to be first time homeowners. My late husband and I did not have a lot of money, when in fact, we didn't have any money at all, but we did have mustard seed faith. Our hope was in the promise God gave to us that if we would live for Him that He would give us the desires of our heart. Therefore, we went out to look for our house. I realize that for some of you, this may sound like poor planning and no preparation on our part but we were new converts taught to believe the Lord for everything so we did. The Lord blessed us to find the home we could be happy in so we planted our seed into it. Now do not laugh but our seed was five dollars and twenty-three cents, it was all my husband had in his pocket at the time. *Hebrews 11:1 says, Now faith is the substance of things hoped for* and the substance was his pocket change. Soon after obtaining the mortgage, the Lord blessed us to come up with the required down payment. Things seemed to be going along just fine and with the next step being the closing process our excitement was heightened. Our lawyer was competent to handle the arrangements so we agreed to pay him a fee of two hundred dollars, which was a fair price. The rest of the scripture says, *the evidence of things not seen.* What we did not see was how we were going to pay our lawyer the two hundred dollars we owed him with the fifty dollars we scraped together. Now Faith.

The day finally came that we were sitting at the table in the county building with the sellers of our house and their lawyer on one side and our lawyer with us on the other side. Everybody was all smiles because we were all getting what we wanted. A lifelong dream fulfilled for us and our hopes were becoming a reality. After we shook hands with the sellers, they left the room. Oh, if only we could have left the room too, but we had the final piece of the process to fulfill. If you have ever experienced that uncomfortable silence when you don't know what to say or do, then you know how we felt. How do you tell someone who worked hard on your behalf that all you had was a quarter of his fee? The silence was deadening but it only lasted for about five minutes (seemed longer). My husband could not delay any longer and as he was about to speak, our lawyer took a small manila envelope from his pocket and said "by the way the bank overpaid the sellers one hundred fifty six dollar and fifty six cents, would you like me to keep this for my fee? The evidence we could not see was in our lawyer's pocket all the time and with the money we had, the Lord manifested His promise of hope toward us. Both of us were shouting and dancing all around that room but no one knew it but us. That was our home for ten years and then the Lord blessed us again but that's another story.

Not to put a damper on all of this but there are some situations where no matter how much you hope, they will not live. That is when it was not one of God's promises for you. When we put our hope and trust in the things we desire over what His will is, life is gone. The only reason it lingers on is that we keep applying the shock paddles when it should flat line out. Look at all the wasted energy expended for something that is short lived. Go ahead, pull the plug, and let it die naturally, with the dignity it deserves. We will not receive everything we hope for if our desires are not edifying Christ. Let us seek to put all our hope into the Promise of Hope, which is the substance of life and who, guarantees everlasting results which is life everlasting.

CONTEMPLATIVE MOMENTS

1. Your faith moment was?

2. Did you ever give up hope?

3. What were the results of your hope journey?

The Gas Cap

Have you ever heard a word or two spoken in your subconscious that was so farfetched to anything you were thinking at the time that it made you wonder how it is relevant to your life today? Well, it happened to me as I sat at work the day we were to pick up our new used automobile. I was so excited about getting the new car because the one we had was literally falling apart and we needed some dependable transportation. The words I heard were Gas Cap. Ok, it does have something to do with the event but it is not the first thing you would focus on pertaining to a vehicle. Your assumption is that the car has one and that is that. However, the words were so clear that I could not deny what I heard. No words in front or behind it, just the two words alone. I even repeated them aloud trying to figure out the significant of it so I returned to my work and the thought was forgotten for awhile. *1 Corinthians 12:8 For to one is given by the Spirit the word of wisdom; to another the word of knowledge by the same Spirit.*

The word of knowledge was another gift revealed to me, and I heard it.

As we drove to the dealership our conversation was about

everything but what I heard. Maybe I should mention what time of the year it was as it will be noteworthy later in the story. It was a cold, snowy day in January with about two feet of the white stuff on the ground and it just happened to be Buffalo, NY. Buffalo, known affectionately as the Snow Belt capital of the world but we do have nice weather more often than people may think. I hope that this will help you to visualize what we were dealing with on that day.

When we arrived at the showroom, another salesman told us that our sales representative was currently unavailable so he would finish the transaction. After completing the necessary paperwork, we promptly took possession of our new automobile and went merrily on our way. Take heed to the word or words put in your spirit because they come to help you avoid difficulties down the road. Down the road, we went to the gas station and when my husband started to pump gas into the tank, he noticed something was missing. Aha, it was the gas cap; you know that thing that every car normally has. Well, our car did not have one so back to the dealer we went. In less than an hours' time the attitude of the salesperson had changed drastically and it was not for the better. My husband told him about the missing gas cap and he made a little scene as if we were trying to get something for nothing. His next suggestion really was out of line and a little disrespectfully. He told us if we want another one that we would have to go out into the back lot where there was about three feet of snow and get it from one of the cars there. This upset us greatly because we had just spent a substantial amount of money with them. Thankfully by this time we were approached by the person who originally assisted us with the car purchase and we were able to communicate what transpired in his absence. He said he was aware of the missing cap and he had one in his desk drawer but forgot to tell anyone about it. Two words were all we needed which the Lord had spoken to me and I heard it. The Lord will make a way of escape even from frustration and confrontation.

What a Wonderful God we Serve.

CONTEMPLATIVE MOMENTS

1. Have you ever heard something that helped later?

2. Do you have any spiritual gifts?

3. Tell of one experience

Closed Door

When the door closes, it may not always be the Lord shutting it. You may have to put up a little resistance against the enemy. We always take for granted that the Lord closes every door but the enemy is more likely to attempt to keep good things from us. In 1Samuel 30: 1-8 David thought the battle was over because so many things and people had come against him. His first consideration was to retreat and hide away. Could he win the fight? It didn't look possible with all the odds against him. He had to encourage himself and ask the Lord should he pursue what was lost. The answer was yes, go after it overtake it and bring back what the enemy stole from you.

A closed door does not always mean there is no entry. It reminds me of the friends of a lame man. They heard Jesus was in the house and they needed to be there too. When the men saw no way in through the windows and doors, they did the next best thing – tore the roof off. It was a little radical but their friend was worth the extra effort to be healed. I love the fact that a closed door was not allow to stop hope for a miracle.

Paul and Silas had to deal with a closed door when they were in prison for setting the captives free with a salvation word. Stuck in the inner prison with their feet shackled and surrounded on every hand they decided to pray and give praise to the Liberator of all liberators for all the prisoners to hear. The praise became so intense that it cause an earthquake opening the prison doors and loosed all the shackles. When the keeper of the prison saw the doors open, he almost killed himself believing all who were inside had escaped but instead he was freed with all his family who were not even there. Praise opened the doors.

Should we close the doors on some situations in our life? Only the ones that are not profitable or that celebrate our lives. Do you know which ones they are? Yes you do. I know personally the ones I need to close for my own good. If the associations are impeding your spiritual growth and are not leading into your designed destiny, drop it. Close that door. I pray God gives us all the wisdom and the strength to end the cycle of opening and closing the same going no way door, getting that foot out of way slamming it shut, losing the key. And take that hand off the doorknob.

COMTEMPLATIVE MOMENTS

1. Did the Lord ever close doors on or for you?

2. Was it difficult for you to leave it closed?

3. What were the results of this action?

Heartstrings

My objective with this story is to be a help to those of us who have had relationships that didn't end up the way we thought it should. Right now, we are supposed to be living that happily ever after life with the person we chose to live it with an emphasis on who we chose. Perhaps I am not the one to give advice on this subject because I still consider myself a novice although I was married for thirty years to one man. Nevertheless, a relationship is a relationship no matter if it's with one person or many. Life is teaching us many lessons about how we interact with each other as we learn what makes the other person tick. Funny but at this stage of my life who knew I would have to deal with relationship issues because I was in the best one of my life. It was love at first sight or something like that. The chemistry was all over the place but I was young figuring it couldn't be that but it was. I didn't go looking for this love, it just happened to come walking down the street and found me: *Proverbs 18:22 Whoso findeth a wife findeth a good thing, and obtaineth favour of the LORD.* Sometimes our hearts get attached with another heart early in life and it can last for a lifetime. When it ends and it will; there seems to be a few loose ends, those heartstrings that seeks to be tied to another heart and this can take place when we make wrong choices all in the name of love. Oh, those crazy heartstrings and they are crazy... There are so many reasons we use in the pursuit of a relationship but they are not always the right ones. If you don't mind I will list a few or maybe some, okay I will list a lot so we can all decide whether it is man or woman where we find ourselves somewhere in the number.

1. My biological clock is ticking-tick tick tock.
2. It is taking too long, it might not happen I have to settle.
3. If I can't be with the one I love, I will love the one I am with.
4. He is cute, rich kind of cute, muscles kind of cute.
5. She's fine, shapely kind of fine, can cook a little kind of fine.
6. He/she says all the right words that make you feel the right way.
7. He/she says they are a Christian.
8. I am lonely plain and simple.
9. Nobody's perfect and anybody is better than nobody.
10. Yes, I see the warning signs but he/she can change.
11. I just love him/her and I can make him/her love me.
12. The rabbit died or the stick turned blue or pink

I am going to stop here while the list is still on the nice side. Another reason I will cease is that I don't have enough time to continue as I have already added more and need to move on. If your reason is not on this list, it is only because you are not being honest with yourself or maybe you have been sheltered which can be a good thing. Then again perhaps this just has been your experience. No relationship so no heartstrings. If you want to move to the next story in the book it's okay as this may not be for you. Nevertheless, for others I hope I have gotten your interest as I try to make sense of how we get our heartstrings tangled, yanked on, or easily broken. This is a universal situation on how relationships are lackadaisically initiated by one person, who then leaves the other person longing for more which is not forthcoming. In other words, someone plays with the heart while someone else get his or her heart played with. Although it might not be done intentionally or maliciously to hurt, it can. I thought this would be an account on how we get our hearts hurt and a bashing of the predators of the heart but it seems to have evolved into the lessons we learn so we will not have to repeat the class. I hope that many of you think the way I do which is realizing life is full of lessons intended to move us on to the next level of maturity. If we don't learn a lesson the first time, it might come around again, and if it does it may be just as hard to get over. So hopefully we can use the first experience as our cheat sheet to not repeat the process.

I did an opinion poll concerning heartstrings of my family, friends, and co-workers and received some great thought provoking comments from both men and women with varied backgrounds and experiences. It was not really a question that I posed as much as what came to mind when they heard or thought of the words "heart strings." The comments were as varied as the people I surveyed and very inspiring. These are the powerful comments I received.

Someone that is tied to your heart - someone you care for.

> Yvonne M in heaven now

I think of attachments like soul ties. When you get in a relationship or have relations, you leave a part of you behind. How long is your heartstring?

> Mike H.

Sometimes feels unbreakable. Can be a stronghold. Should be connected, attached, or felt at all times with a higher awareness that gives peace and truth with honest guidance, Jesus Christ Himself.

> Sharon O.

The connection to who God is in our life. The connection to who God is in your life

> Regina J.

Attracted to those who are attracted to you. Like the attention and special treatment given to you through the feelings are not the same.

> Terry J

Heartstrings are the feeling one display toward their love one.

> Charles S

Blood vessels - Funnel in your life - through vessels in the heart. Carrying things to and from the heart. People attached to your heart, nurturing us with what we need flowing in and out.

   Chauntrell W.

In the past, medical experts believed that a "heart string" was a major tendon or nerve that supported the heart. Therefore, when I think of that concept, I reflect upon my relationship with the Lord. When I allow the Holy Spirit in my heart, I am more receptive to the sensation of the tug and pull of my heartstrings. As a result, that pull gently confirms His love for me, comforts me when I am lonely, and reminds me of the sacrifice that He made just for me. Because of that, I want to please Him through my obedience, my worship, my life, and my love for others.

   Leslie J.

My heart and spirit warms me when I wake up every morning knowing that I have at least two people who love me unconditionally.

   Danielle R.

Love – Somebody you are crazy about and they got you.

   Gregory B.

Someone or something that is attached to you by an invisible string and is attached to your mind and/or heart.

Michael T III

The emotional tethers to your heart that can be pulled for negative or positive results

Raymond B.

To me when I think about heartstrings it reminds me of the dealing with months of being uncomfortable, leading up to being in excruciating pain, agony, and tiredness only to hear that faint or strong cry and see that little face of someone that you carried for months......it was all worth it......heartstrings.

La Tasha J

When I hear the term heartstrings I think of my children when they were little.... they consumed my thoughts.... I thought when they became older this would change but it hasn't.... lol

Niecie (Sharon D)

There is an instrument called the heart, and it does come with strings. And each heart is equipped with its own unique songs to play, pre-programmed by the Father for His purpose. Now the strings on the instrument do not come finely tuned... but in time, they are tuned to perfection by our trials, worship, ups and downs, praise, perseverance, faith and love unconditional.

Kenny D

What does heartstrings mean to me?

Affection for someone who gained access to the innermost vessels of your emotional being and whether they are still there physically or not, continue to be attached to your consciousness. You still love them.

Gwendolyn

It's not always easy to cut those strings when you are using dull scissors and that is to say, it is not always an unpleasant experience to have loved and lost because for once in your life you made a difference in the life of someone else. You really mattered. However, if the predator of the heart is you, what goes around comes around, and it may be you dangling from one of those strings trying to get loose. Please do not let it be your fate. Michael T, one of my grandsons, is the youngest contributor to this story which shows everyone can relate to heartstrings. Thanks for your contributions. Love it!

CONTEMPLATIVE MOMENTS

1. What does heartstrings mean to you?

2. Did you learn anything from the experience?

3. Share with someone

Seven Times a Wife

Jesus met a woman at Jacob's well and had a very interesting conversation with her. He was tired and thirsty as any man would be after traveling from city to city teaching all who would hear His word. While the disciples were buying food in town, He sat down at the well to rest. A Samaritan woman came to draw water and Jesus asked her for a drink. Bewilderment entered her mind because she knew the Jews had no association with anyone outside of their culture especially someone from Samaria and a woman at that.

Jesus then told her about the forever thirst-quenching water He was offering. It was from the well that would never run dry. *John 4:14 But whosoever drinketh of the water that I shall give him shall never thirst; but the water that I shall give him shall be in him a well of water springing up into everlasting life.* When the woman asked for a drink of that water, the Lord asked her to bring her husband to Him. With my spiritual ear, I can hear her saying to herself, what does He know about me; I am not wearing any rings. Her response was she didn't have a husband. Jesus said she did well by saying she was husband less and in fact she had five

The bible doesn't mention the husbands again with reference

to what her relationship may have been with each of them nor does it comment on any of their personalities, flaws or ambitions. The narrative was about a Gentile woman hearing the word, believing and accepting it then witnessing to others about a man who can give eternal life. I would like to concentrate on the Husband issue and how it is to have more than one husband yet only married once. Again, I can hear you say, what is she talking about now? My account is about something that may seem a little peculiar but we are a peculiar people who have unique experiences that have extraordinary results.

What is it like being the Wife of seven Husbands each one having ever so slightly different characteristics? No, he did not have multiple personalities. He was one man that exhibited various Christ like attributes as he was elevated from new level to new level and a higher height to a higher height.

We entered into matrimony for many reasons and may have had different agendas, but whatever the reason was at the time, Leon and I got married. This is about being a wife times seven.

Unsaved Wife.
Husband One

We met as teenagers and within three years we were Husband and Wife. We were also teenage parents and wanted to do the right thing. Sometimes the right thing is for all the wrong reasons and for us it may have been too soon. It was a struggle for us to handle that much responsibility. We both had dreams and aspirations of what we wanted our lives to be and becoming adults before we had gain maturity was not one of our life's goals. Husband One had to deal with being a breadwinner with three other people to support and having to face the world not fully equipped for the challenge. There was a spiritual side to Husband One. He was a good man with a huge heart but not a totally committed servant of God. Without the Godhead in our lives, it was like the blind leading the blind and I was willing to follow. He liked to party and enjoyed much of what went with it, so did I. We had to be grown ups and set a good example for the children we brought into this world and that created tension and strain on the relationship. We were not quite ready. Husband One was a great person but after years of us trying to feel our way through with no help or guidance; we were on our way to divorce court. There were many arguments and disagreements to the point where it seemed hard for us to forget the inappropriate words spoken in the heat of anger. But the scripture speaks about letting our words be few and seasoned with grace like in *Colossians 4:6 to let your speech be always with grace, seasoned with salt, that ye may know how ye ought to answer every man.* Sometimes it's better not to speak at all because once the words are spoken, they are in the air. This is where a soft answer would be appropriate to turn away any lingering hurtful words as found in *Proverbs 15:1 a soft answer turneth away wrath: but grievous words stir up anger.* Believe me when I say your mate does not need to know everything that is on your mind yet at the appropriate time you should be able to talk about anything. Why would you want to launch out with intentional hurt on your mind? That is your soul mate, your better half, your main squeeze, the love of your life and the one you chose to be with. Communication is one thing you can't afford to let slip because if it does you could lose some of the trust factor involved in building a strong marriage. Watch your words and only use the ones that will promote good marital health.

The issues of life were making our relationship difficult. In addition, it wasn't easy to adjust to life with a spouse and children when you are a child yourself. I went from my momma's house to my Husband's house without learning about me. Neither one of us really wanted to call it quits but what else could prevent this from happening. Jesus happened. I appreciated the television ministry that eventually got his attention when his back was against the wall cornered on all sides. At some point in time we have to get tired of ourselves messy as it is. Husband One the unsaved man got tired of himself, walked out the door and in walked Husband Two. In others words he was saved and what a ripple effect that caused.

Saved Wife.
Husband Two

It was an amazing transformation because outwardly One and Two looked so similar; you would have thought they were the same person. Roman 12:2 states that the transformation is a renewing of the mind and David asked the Lord to create in him a clean heart and to renew a right spirit within him. That was exactly what Leon did and at that moment, I had a new Husband. I became a Wife for a second time to a changed man. Let me tell you that the old man had surely changed and I beheld all things become new. Husband Two did not desire the things of the world nor did he want to participate in its activities that had once given him so much pleasure. His very appearance did indeed take on a different look as the light of Christ began to shine brighter he even sounded differently. There was no new wine in old wineskins and there was no old Leon in this new Husband. Now I was still Wife One and was not quite ready to let my life go. You see there was still a lot of living I wanted to do. I wasn't sure if I wanted the lifestyle or commitment of this new man in my life. Therefore, I continued to live my life and for a while, it seemed to work. Husband Two was not going to let me sway him into giving up the best thing he ever found or maybe I should say the One that found him (salvation). Funny because I thought I was the best in his life and for a while I believed I was. He now had peace of mind although he still had the same problems and situations that really had not changed but for the first time in our marriage, unequally yoked were we but he was praying for me. I can testify to the scripture in *1 Corinthians 7:14 for the unbelieving Husband is sanctified by the Wife, and the unbelieving Wife is sanctified by the Husband: else were your children unclean; but now are they holy.* It was through his prayers and belief that if God could change him He would do the same for me and He did, I was saved. Now that was an experience I will never forget becoming a new creature myself letting the Lord change me too. Because of the relationship that Leon and I had, I didn't want to be left behind. Was that a good reason to be saved, I don't know but it was reason enough for me. I remember the night I received the Holy Ghost as one of the best experience of my life. I could see a radiant glow all over me like brand new. I became Wife Two saved Wife and our children became holy. We finally had a meaningful respect for each other and knew what it was to really love each other for the first time. There was a unity of our bodies, souls, and minds with a real knowledge and understanding of what our wedding vows meant. Marriage is a work in progress, not tedious but effort has to be made by both partners to maintain continuity and balance. Having common interests helped to build the friendship and yes our marriage was a friendship first. You know I like you and you like me. We could see the relationship making an upward spiral the more we got to know each other again in this new life. A beautiful journey was at hand and I was chosen to make it with him.

While going through some of Leon's writing I came across his testimony in his own words and wanted to share it with you.

Oh taste and see that the Lord is good! It was November or in that general area of the year that the Lord gave me the mind to be saved. The year was 1976 and many things had happened that year that caused me to seek for positive answers. After watching the 700 club my life was changed. I made the first step by calling their helpline after which I was prayed for, repented of my sins and began to even feel the difference in my life.

The enemy wasn't pleased with my new spirituality and attempted to tempt me with many things. Thank God that instead of giving in I began to seek God even more.

For a short while, I joined my family's church and eventually didn't return because after attending a revival at a sanctified church I realized that I needed more than to have my name on the roll. After being filled with the Holy Ghost that year I knew that I would never return to the Baptist church where I had received the right hand of fellowship.

After I joined Deliverance Temple, Gwen was saved shortly after and we became full-fledged members of the church. We sang in the choir, served as ushers and I was appointed as a trustee and then a deacon of the church.

I am always glad to find and include any of his writings, although I may be repeating myself. I love having Leon's contribution to any story since he was such a great writer and this was from his perspective.

A Trustee/Deacon's Wife.
Husband Three

I know you are saying right now, she tricked me. She made it seem this would be some shady little gossip story about someone who just couldn't seem to find the right man. Please don't think I'm throwing off on anyone who has been involved in more than one marriage because I'm not. We all look for happiness but sometimes we settle for less than what we deserve just to have someone in our lives. This is to the single women who think they need a man to validate them when they are incredible and capable of anything all by themselves. That's another story so back to the one at hand. By this time I was about to meet my third Husband. The difference with this man was his eagerness to learn all he could about the new life he found, eating the Word like a little bird fresh out the shell hungry for food. I remember him sitting on the front seat of the church feasting on God's word. This man became wholeheartedly and fully engulfed in the Lord, a willing vessel filled with the spirit of God. There were times that I felt like I had lost him to the church and I can honestly say it eventually happened. The alternative could have been worst if I had lost him to the world with all of its enticements. Through his faithfulness to God and the church, the pastor chose him to be a deacon, which made me Wife Three. This was another level for him and me as well. A new responsibility and level of anointing was essential to meet the requirement of this office. *1Timothy 3:8-13 describes this level of ministry: 8.Likewise must the deacons be grave, not double-tongued, not given to much wine, not greedy of filthy lucre; 9Holding the mystery of the faith in a pure conscience. 10And let these also first be proved; then let them use the office of a deacon, being found blameless. 11Even so must their wives be grave, not slanderers, sober, faithful in all things. 12Let the deacons be the Husbands of one Wife, ruling their children and their own houses well. 13For they that have used the office of a deacon well purchase to themselves a good degree, and great boldness in the faith, which is in Christ Jesus.* Husband Three was on the scene for a season but little did either of us know his time was limited and soon to be replaced. While he was with me, he was evolving, learning, changing, studying to show himself approved unto God, a workman that need not be ashamed rightly dividing the word of truth. Then he received a call he could not refuse and he was gone. Husband Three the deacon stepped out and in stepped Husband Four.

A Minister's Wife.
Husband Four

The bible says that many are called but few chosen and because of that, this man had an entirely different persona than the previous ones, which had to do with a higher call to that of a chosen one. You could see a preparedness or a getting readiness in him. Husband Four chosen to accept the call of a minister of God and preach the Lord's word to all with open ears to hear and willing hearts to receive. As I write this story, I wonder how many people will actually relate to it. There may even be some men who can see themselves and say this could be my story of transformation. With each level of righteousness came more responsibility, another set of tests to pass and a greater love for the Master and entitlement to His authority. Husband Four had gained more power that was made evident in every area of his life and it engulfed me as well. A minister's Wife, imagine that.

His trial sermon was on a Friday night with two other brothers chosen to serve the Lord to a higher degree. They called themselves the 3 Musketeers. The training was on the job with Pastor Lincoln Williams Sr. as the well-versed and able mentor. Leon received his ministerial license on May 7 1989. There was a certain comradery that existed among the men who were in attendance at that time. Some were ministers in training and there were others that didn't know this would be their destiny. To see them interact with each other, you would think all they were doing was either arguing or debating. But it was more like a challenge to encourage each other to study the word and to learn all they could and would. Again I felt as if I was losing him but it was a privilege and honor to lose him to the Lord for we both benefited, nothing lost all to gain. There stood my fourth Husband, to stay because where else could he go. My eyes were opened to a new reality and I was seeing things with a whole new perspective. Leon was learning all he needed to make that transition into Husband Five a smooth shift, now being able to perform all the ordinances of church. A higher level of anointing was radiating which made the next step to take easy. Another changed man which made preaching easier also. Here came Husband Five.

An Elder's Wife.

Husband Five

With this new Husband, life was just ever so slightly different. It would have gone unnoticed if I didn't have the gift of discernment. The Lord thrust us into the inner working of ministry with me having a bird eye view of yet another amazing conversion. Like Solomon, this Husband was blessed with an incredible amount of wisdom knowing how to come in and go out among the people. He stood flat footed without whooping or hollering to deliver the unadulterated word of God. Being bible taught and without the advantage of any outside schooling, he earned his degree of higher learning by seeking God's face for everything and was ordained an elder on August 9, 1992. All things were possible as the level of faith rose from that of a mustard seed to a mighty tree reaching to heaven's throne. I have to say it was just slightly different because without realizing it preparation made for yet another Husband's departure. I could see that shepherd spirit manifesting itself, as our pastor would leave him in charge of the church often. He had a confidence in Leon that the flock was safe in his care. On September 13, 1995, he began a home bible study, which was the beginning of the beginning. New Husband one who cared for God's little lambs was on the way and that would make six.

One Sunday after church, a mother who unknowingly had a prophetic word greeted me and also brought confirmation of another elevation. She said that I would soon become a pastor's Wife. Silly me, I thought it couldn't be to another man because my Husband had no intention on being that. I was not ready to leave my comfort zone for uncharted territory – not me. However, that gift of discernment I mentioned earlier let me know it to be true. Circumstances happened which encouraged him to leave and set in motion another realm of obedience. All the trials and tribulations we went through previously were just a set up for this transition out of our comfort zone into that uncharted territory – not me, yes me. Husbands Six are you really coming?

A Pastor's Wife.
Husband Six

I hope you realize that with each new Husband, I became a new Wife. My growth could be measured as well as his in the areas needed for my role within the ministry. As Husband Six settled into his new persona, I did, too. The change was evident in both of us as we mature to face the new challenges and responsibilities of this office. We were in a different world, on a different level doing different things with different mates. Talk about having to learn each other again – we had to. Again, I was losing him, hey, I think I said this before. I tried not to complain because it was a good thing. The skills this Husband had for that time and place, was the result of the preparation period which turned into the release of his destiny. It was his time.

We found a building and converted it into a very nice church with the help of many friends. Leon was able to use many of his building skills and did much of the design work as well. The bible education passed on to him from Husband Five made preaching easy and he did it with such grace that I was impressed with him. There was one Sunday while preaching he began to quote a scene from Othello, that's right I said he quoted it and it impressed me to no end. His education was in many venues all without a degree. He was a very intelligent man. It must be evidenced by now that I loved this man.

For two years Husband Six was living his dream, with passion, with diligence and faith. During this time we purchased a building on Broadway that is currently pastored by our oldest son Terry. Husband Six even lived one of his desires, which was full time ministry because in August of 1999, we found out his time was really ending but unlike all my other Husbands, the transformation would be from dimension to dimension (cancer) forever. And in July 2000, our time was over and Husband Six moved on for real, the Lord took him home. But I had the privilege of watching the Lord prepare a boy into manhood into maturity a thirty-three-year process. It was our life together. Through the entire process, the Lord was preparing me for yet another Husband, Husband Seven.

The Maker's Wife
Husband Seven

What can I say about Husband Seven except, He does not have to learn my ways, He knows my ways. He knew me before I existed, awesome. With Him there is no question about His love, *1 John 4:18 there is no fear in love but perfect love cast out fear.*

Will He change or evolve in any way? *Malachi 3:6 says I am the Lord, I change not.* My Husband is now my Lord for He inclines His ear to the widows and entreats our requests with mercy and care. There has been such peace and comfort in this time of the journey. Although I miss Leon what I miss the most was knowing I would see him at the end of the day, feeling his arms around me, hearing him call my name, seeing his face as he is seeing mine. The touch is next, so gentle and tender yet, the firm holds which embraces, drawing me in closer and closer. I can feel his breathe as he would breathe warm breaths down the back of my neck sending shivers down my spine. More of what I miss is while I am in his embrace feeling the beat of our hearts, as they became rhythmically one. I miss knowing there was at least one person that loved me unconditional and still wanted to be with me. This is a difficult process to go through when you lose a loved one and you were not finish loving them. I miss my Husband because I always felt there would never be another love like his. That was something I had always told myself because I realize that I may not be the easiest person to live with but who really is. I heard today that some of us are still attached to dead people, meaning that we are living our lives trying to please them or keep their memory alive and making them bigger than life to maintain an illusion of existence that is no longer there. By making this statement, I will have to admit that I was guilty but no one should judge me on this but God because you never know what you would do until you are in the same situation. Transition is not easy to make but what choice do you have but to make it. Life is full of changes. That is what makes it interesting. The Lord created us for change, that's why our lives are constantly move forward even when we try to hold it back. Then the Lord told me something new.

The scripture in *Isaiah 54:5 says for thy Maker is thine Husband; the Lord of host is his name; and the Redeemer the Holy One of Israel: The God of the whole earth shall he be called.* Prepared and ready for marriage to God, like the five wise virgins on the way to be filled with the oil of joy to go into the marriage with my bridegroom. He is always there and now I see that He is my One Husband.

The New Wife.
Husband Eight

No, my count is not off, seven times a Wife. Nevertheless, the Lord is not done for He has arranged for me to have a new Husband of His choosing and His design. Husband Eight will be a new beginning for both of us. The rest of my life will I spend with him. God will not take something away without blessing us all over again. We may have met and then again, we may meet one day for the first time but whatever the circumstances, it will be our destiny.

At the time of this writing the new Husband is not here yet but I believe the promise of God and that's enough for me. I believe this will be.

Husband One through Six was the love of my life, Husband Seven is pure love, and Husband Eight will be God's love to me. Feel the love, His gift to us.

Footnote:

How many people get to meet and marry their best friend and have it last for thirty years? There are not many. How many people find an unconditional love, one that sees your weaknesses but builds up your strengths? Not many find it but it is out there. How many people have a perfect love with all its imperfections? I did and I will have it again, for God said my latter would be greater than my former and my former was great.

Thank you Lord – Number One Husband.

CONTEMPLATIVE MOMENT

What does marriage mean to you?

After All
He Has Done

In one of life's moments, I was dealing with what I will call a broken heart, yes a broken heart. In a brief moment of feeling sorry for myself, I had a little lapse of mind and dared to say that Jesus did not have to go through any heartache, although He said He knows how we feel. Who would hurt His heart and the answer came so quickly that it almost knocked me off my feet. Can you guess who the culprit responsible for His hurt is? We are, me included with selfish design and self-promoting agendas. He shows us His unconditional love, shows us his good intentions, shows us how much He cares and we make light of it. God is compassionate, sympathetic, and empathetic through Jesus Christ His son. He is the one that heals the hurt and brings comfort in times of pain. *Romans 5:8 But God commendeth his love toward us, in that, while we were yet sinners, Christ died for us.*

Well, what do you know, God has feelings too, only He knows how to keep them in check. We tug at His heartstrings when we complain about how His plan does not line up with ours. If I can give you some advice, it would be this, be careful what you ask for because you just might get it, not His plan but through our stubborn will. There are many times when the getting is not worth the having. When I received that answer, it shut my mouth because my hurt came as the result of moving too fast in the wrong direction and with the wrong person. Heartstrings are sometimes a little difficult to unravel but we tug at the ties connected to our Lord's heart with such disregard.

Nevertheless, let us focus further on what hurts God's heart. *2Cor 4:17 states, for our light affliction, which is but for a moment, worketh for us a far more exceeding and eternal weight of glory; which* tells me my little hurt is just that, one little hurt. But if we were to multiply that by the millions and millions who don't consider God's hurt at all when they turn their backs by saying there is no god, and decide not to believe or trust Him and take His grace and mercy for granted.

When Satan was puffed up and caught up in whom he thought he was, he then convinced a third of heaven that he was all that plus a bag of chips in the yellow bag. I do not think we could handle what God must have felt in seeing His creation deny Him as sovereign. My spiritual eye can see one of His tears creating grand canyons and the mighty rivers that runs through the earth. In my spiritual ear, I hear His sigh which are the four winds blowing in every direction and His cry would be the echoes that still reverberate in the valleys low.

Why do we put our Lord through all this knowing He has feelings? *Exodus 3:7 And the LORD said, I have surely seen the affliction of my people, which are in Egypt, and have heard their cry by reason of their taskmasters; for I know their sorrows.* If God had to turn His back on His own son and let darkness fill the earth because He could not look at how much Jesus had to suffer for us, so why would we want to inflict unwarranted frustration when it is not called for.

Let us get ourselves together and realize that the suffering of this world cannot compare to the joy there in paradise. Pull yourselves up by your bootstraps and endure these light afflictions as a good soldier. *1Corinthians 10:13 There hath no temptation taken you but such as is common to man: but God is faithful, who will not suffer you to be tempted above that ye are able; but will with the temptation also make a way to escape, that ye may be able to bear it.* Jesus made the way of escape so you can avoid the pitfalls of life and not suffer unnecessary pain. *2Thessalonians 3:5 And the Lord direct your hearts into the love of God, and into the patient waiting for Christ.*

Be patient trusting the plan from above and as our Father is mindful of our feelings, we should be mindful of His. If we will do better, we will have better and His best should always get better.

CONTEMPLATIVE MOMENTS

1. What has the Lord done for you later?

2. Do you complain without realizing it?

3. What positive words do speak over yourself?

Emancipation Road

While performing one of my duties at work, much has happened while at work, I came across the address of one the vendors I was billing. It struck a chord in me that I could not let go of right away. As I wrote it down - thoughts of what it really meant flooded my mind. It is Emancipation Road. When a story idea comes to me or presents itself to me as they often do, I will look up the meaning of the words. I was surprised at some of the definitions and I didn't go to the bible yet. With only the definitions and a few scriptures, usually I could have this story written and be done in a day. No way will this one be that easily. Like I said, the stories I write present themselves and my emancipation comes from writing them down to share with others. You see I am also on this freedom road and each leg of the journey brings me closer to the Emancipator Himself, Jesus Christ. With every stroke of the pen or keyboard, I am completing one of the tasks set before me for we all have something that is pressed upon us to be accomplished - mine is to write and to focus on what will lead me to the next tier of ministry. Here's a little praise break moment.

To emancipate is to set free from bondage, restraints, fritters, and hindrances. This list is lengthier than this but for now let us deal with these. The road to total freedom is not an easy one to travel. There are rest stops on this journey. Which one of us might not need a break from problems every now and then? Consider this: we can also call a rest area our comfort zones but we are not always limitation free. On occasion we may attempt to build a lean-to in these areas when we should only put up a portable hammock or even a folding chair. Eventually the trip will have to continue with us leaving our own self-made security zone to venture on to the freedom path. You see there are steps on this route that will require forward movement to achieve liberation in God.

To achieve the ultimate freedom, we must unload the weights or chains that the enemy so nicely provides and we unwittingly accept as our lot in life. While ministering to a young woman, my spiritual eye saw what look like clothespins attached to her. As I was trying to knock them off the Spirit said if she would run, they would fall off. The clothespins actually represented the weight of life's struggles that were trying to hinder her progress. A simple yet powerful act of faith to run although it seemed foolish was all it would take to be free. Paul stated that we must run this race with patience knowing who is the author and finisher of our faith. It is the simple things asked of us to do that may seem too silly to work. However, the bible says the Lord takes the foolish things to confound the wise. Faith first believed then conceived. Praise Him on that one.

The process of emancipation requires faith in God,

dependence on His word, His instruction and courage to follow through without being able to see more a than a few feet in front of you and most time not that far. Trust what I say or better still; trust the Lord has the journey mapped out with detour and stop signs in strategic places to help avoid hazards along the way. The road is narrow yet wide enough for the journey made for light traveling. This is a reminder just like the one you hear at the airport asking you not to agree to watch or carry anyone else's baggage. Folks may look at you and see how easily and unencumbered you move down the road. The only reason would be you have given your baggage to the baggage handler Himself. Don't heed to those who want you to watch or carry their stuff because they see you have room. You are not a baggage cart. Holler!

Emancipation Road is an open path with many twist and turns. At times, you may travel it two by two or three by three but at your own pace with different rest stops or off ramps for each runner in the race. This means, occasionally we have someone who helps us to achieve a certain leg of the journey then moves on leaving us. Just be encouraged to run on a little further. The common factor should be the attitude we all carry down the path toward freedom, which is the attitude of praise and gratitude to the foundation builder, map planner and journey instructor, Jesus.

Free at last. We can dance with this one!

CONTEMPLATIVE MOMENTS

1. What road do you see ahead of you?

2. What roadblocks are holding you up?

3. How can you travel more freely?

Home Is Where the Heart Is

Have you ever had a longing to go home to a place you believe exist but have never been before? I have that longing but it may be because there have been so many major changes in my life. One of them was leaving everything familiar to me and moving to another city. The Lord has shown favor in so many ways that I am in awe of Him. When I needed a place to live he did not give me just any old apartment but a beautiful one situated on a lake. I have all I need to make me feel at home and I am comfortable here. However, when I think about home it is nothing like this. Recently I have heard a sermon referring to having thoughts of wanting to leave this earthly dwelling. Sometimes the pressures of life get you down and causes you to have an earnest heartfelt desire for a better existence. Now the bible tells us of a home, one we do not have to build, the Master prepared for us. Man has never touched it, yet the design is perfectly suited for us and made to the exact specification for our habitation. The master architect drafts the blueprint and we all know He was also a carpenter by trade. The bible also tells us that there are many dwelling places there and they are not just big fancy houses but mansions and since we know what mansions look like here on earth, imagine the detail taken to the ones in heaven because our Savoir is a detailed kind of God. *John 14:1-3 1. Let not your heart be troubled: ye believe in God, believe also in me. 2. In my Father's house are many mansions: if it were not so, I would have told you. I go to prepare a place for you. 3. And if I go and prepare a place for you, I will come again, and receive you unto myself; that where I am, there ye may be also.*

Visualize the most beautiful sight you have ever seen and I can guarantee our heavenly home will be better than that only because His word says so. There is a phenomenon called God's Eye that I am sure you have probably received in an email at one time or another. It is a remarkable sight because it looks like a human eye set out in the heavens. The phenomenon is made of gases and such but in nature many things are not always, what they appear to be. The first time I saw it, I was a little afraid because it appeared to be looking directly at me. It almost proves that His eye does watch over us for protection and guidance making sure we are well taken care of but also seeing all that we do rather it is right or wrong. It seems I have gotten off the original subject of home and wanting to be there but when you allow the Lord to have the reigns, He can steer you in another direction but a connection will be made that makes sense of it in the end. *1 Peter 3:12 for the eyes of the Lord are over the righteous, and his ears are open unto their prayers: but the face of the Lord is against them that do evil.* God never ignores our prayers when we entreat Him with our petition for direction and guidance. He watches our every move and offers a path if we need to know which way to go. We get sidetracked from our course toward our heavenly home because life throws in a detour or a very large pothole. If we hold fast to the Master's hand and let Him lead as if we were dancing, the turns and spins would be so effortless like the time you danced while standing on your daddy's feet. Memories like that remind me of home.

Home is where the heart is and the older you get the more your heart seems to be content, comfortable and settled some place or any place where your love is. The wanderlust becomes more and more a thing of the past and at the end of the workday or just any day the heart turns toward home for rest from the ordeals, difficulties, and the uncertainty of life. Oh, they tell me of a home. If you will allow me to be myself again, I have to admit that I have been thinking about going home more often these days being concerned with the cares of this world. Although the journey has been very rewarding and interesting with some fantastic twists and turns, my heart still longs to be with the one I love and loves me. Who is that you say, well if you know Him like I do then you know the love of my life. He is the one who makes life possible and all worthwhile.

Please don't think I'm sad or even depressed, but I am hoping for the better place, one that means peace and rest but life, life in another realm in the heaven described in the bible. Streets filled with God's presence, wrapped in His arms, hearing His voice whisper sweet everything's in my ear. Finally resting in comfort feeling secure locked within the protection that is His grace, safe because of His mercy. I don't have a care in the world because this is not my home. *I King 8:39 then hear thou in heaven thy dwelling place, and forgive, and do, and give to every man according to his ways, whose heart thou knowest; for thou, even thou only, knowest the hearts of all the children of men.* With God knowing our heart desires to have all the comforts of home, I must realize that home is where the Lord resides. In His presence is all the solace of home whether here on earth and in heaven, but especially heaven being secure in the knowledge that our names are included in the Lamb's book of life. Home, home, home.

CONTEMPLATIVE MOMENTS

1. Describe home

2. What is your favorite spot in your home?

3. How does home make you feel?

If You Will Wait

This narration is to inform you about a request or prayer you might not want to ask for and that is asking the Lord for patience. Life will bring you enough and then again maybe more than enough reasons to have use the God given patience you already have. But if you want more wait time, ask for it.

There was so many times that if you would have waited, the right things would have happened for you. The NIV bible mentions the word wait about one hundred and thirty six times with the KJV having about one hundred and fifty references. This includes wait, waiting, waited and waiteth. The definition of wait according to the dictionary is to remain or stay in expectation of; await: wait one's turn, to serve the needs of; be in attendance on, wait, there is more. This is the definition for wait out to delay until the termination of. Wow, this woman loves using definitions and scriptures to prove her point. Yes, I do.

To wait does not mean to sit idle waiting for life to happen to you but to use it as an action word. Just sit in one spot and see if you don't start to dry rot and become moldy and if you think the Lord wants or will use you in a state of nothingness doing nothing and of no earthly good to anybody even yourself, you have another thought coming. So this is what I am trying to say. What is wrong with being a little patient and content with where you are now? I doubt if it would hurt much if you didn't have your way all the time.

Sometimes we have a tendency to rush the process by putting the cart before the horse. I did that plenty of times. The Lord has a perfect plan with a divine purpose that will lead to a unique circumstance of enormous proportion with an extraordinary result of great satisfaction. What a mouthful but in others words, He wants to bless you really good and good things come to those that wait on Him.

So what could be wrong with having your marriage arranged by God? Ruth did not fare too bad by having Naomi coach her into her destiny. She got herself a rich husband and I can only imagine that he probably looked good, too. Better than that, imagine being an ancestor of our Savoir Jesus Christ. I encourage you to read the book of Ruth. Please wait. How would it be to have your career guided by the Lord? Noah was instructed on how long, wide, high and deep to build the ark that would save the remnant of civilization following an event that had never happen before or will again. The carpentry work had to be exact which lets us know our God is in the details. To Noah's resume, he could add master carpenter.

We all know of situations where having patience could have prevented some unfortunate results and others that worked out better, for the trying of our faith works patience which will leave us wanting nothing. If there is a connection to all the messages, written so far it would be to trust the Lord no matter what. Most of the time, we should put our trust in Jesus for He will make it all right. If you didn't catch the error in the previous statement, then I challenge you to find it because I know we should strive for perfection in all we do in life. If you need more time, I will give you a few more seconds. Do you give up? I believe you caught it right away and it is the statement beginning with the word -Most. You are good. Why would trusting the Lord most of the time be in error? Because that would infer we may be right twenty percent of the time and we have the solution to our own problems with the limited understanding and far sighted vision we possess. Although we may not have heard or accepted the Lord's answer to wait, be still or even a flat out no, He did answer, even His silence is an answer.

David wanted to build the Lord's temple so he ordered everything needed to build the most elegant and beautiful temple of its time. The prophet Nathan told him to move ahead because it sounded like a good idea. Then the word of the Lord came to Nathan saying although it was a good idea, God rejected him, because of the blood that was on his hands he could not do it. It was then pass down to his son, Solomon, yet still in the family, God chose Solomon to complete the worthy project. Sometimes even a good thing has a waiting period.

My wait is for the greater in my latter that is better than my former like in *Deuteronomy 4:29-30 29 But if from thence thou shalt seek the LORD thy God, thou shalt find him, if thou seek him with all thy heart and with all thy soul. 30When thou art in tribulation, and all these things are come upon thee, even in the latter days, if thou turn to the LORD thy God, and shalt be obedient unto his voice.*

I hope this will encourage all of us to wait for the voice which rings out the instruction that leads to the best solution for any circumstance life has for those called according to His purpose.

Wait on the Lord and again, I say, wait.

CONTEMPLATIVE MOMENTS

1. What are you waiting for?

2. Is it hard or easy?

3. Has the wait been worth the while?

My Mr. Mister Story

This is another instance where I heard from the Lord but this time it was of future events. I like to refer to it as my Mr. Mister story. It's about an experience that most people still have difficulty believing (but I believe and that's all that matters). I always thank the Lord for wanting me to know how much He really cares and wants me to be informed of some of His plans. These events happened during a period of my getting reacquainted with my Savoir Jesus Christ through prayer. The renewing of this relationship was in the fall of 2004. I had become very faithful to pray and the Lord and I had established a dialogue that was like none other I had ever experienced. It made me feel like we were friends like stated in *John 15:15 Henceforth I call you not servants; for the servant knoweth not what his lord doeth: but I have called you friends; for all things that I have heard of my Father I have made known unto you.* In hindsight as I am relating this knowledge to you, I wonder if it was more about trusting in God's plan than what actually happened. With that being said I want to tell you about this amazing story.

Prayer was great and it helped me to get to know an old friend better who has become a great companion in the process. This should be the theme of this story that is getting to know Jesus Christ as a friend. He would talk and I would listen then I would talk and He would answer. During this time I was learning much about my Savoir and how to surrender to His will. In return He communicated to me on a level that was far beyond my expectation *(My thoughts are beyond yours with my ways better than your imagination)*. During this period my intention was not a mercenary one nor a give me this and let me have that kind of prayer but because it was sincere and from the heart, the Lord told me some amazing things.

As well as having fantastic conversation, He was showing me things in dreams and visions. This vision took place at work. While sitting at my desk feeling a little weary my eyes closed for a moment and a face appeared before me. The man was fair skinned with light colored hair and his head was tilted slightly to the side as if he were having a similar vision. Almost as quickly as the face appeared, a name rang in my mind (Mister). When my eyes opened again, the first words out of my mouth were "what was that"? The reply was "you said you wanted a glimpse". This would be a good time to say that much of what the Lord was telling me during that time was about a man in my future. It was all good and I did express that it would be nice to see him if that was possible. So the vision. If it ended there it would have been enough but my Friend didn't let it end there. The Lord also gave me to pray for him and at one point it felt like we were praying together in the spirit realm at least that is my belief. My curiosity was getting the best of me with all this talk about the man and what it really meant yet it still continued.

All this was happening in the fall of 2004 at the same

time I was making plans to attend my church's convocation held in Memphis, Tennessee with Mother Dorothy Dubois (our church mother). I wanted to stay at a certain hotel because it fit into my budget but it was fully booked and the one that was available happen to be more expensive. Knowing how much money I was working with, I asked the Lord why the more costly hotel and He said "I placed you there". After hearing this I started preparing for the trip with the assurance Jesus, my Friend was in control of the situation. All the other arrangements started to fall in line like clockwork which made me more excited about going to Memphis, I had even told Mother Dubois that we were going to enjoy a little luxury when we got there.

The blessings started happening as soon as we arrived in Memphis. I had reserved an economy car in hopes of offsetting the higher room cost but they were all out of them, so to compensate me they gave me a sports vehicle at the same price. Next we had to register for the conference in order to check into our room. Because of some misunderstanding with a disagreeable registrar I was not allow to register with Mother so I stepped out of the room for a moment so as not to make a scene. After a change of staff I was able to continue with the registration process and received an apology for the rudeness shown to me. There was a man sitting at the table next to me and at first I didn't notice him until he attempted to get my attention. He started by asking me several times if we knew each other. Although he did look familiar at that time I couldn't place him. He seemed to be determined to see where we may have met so I told him my name and where I lived. He mentioned some people that both of us knew and that he often came from Detroit to Buffalo to attend different revivals or conferences. We ended our conversation and I began to walk out of the room but was stopped in my tracks as they mentioned his name (Mister). Your name is Mister? He said yes. He seemed to know something about me, too. After telling Mother Dubois about the vision she said it may take a week or a month or years but if this is to go any further it will be exactly what the Lord will have it to be. I am sure we will meet again at the appointed time because what happened is exactly what He showed me.

We serve such an amazing God that even our mind's eye cannot fathom the intricacy of who He really is. We have barely scratched the surface or dug through the first layer of His mindset yet if we are consistent in our pursuit of His excellence and make the utmost sacrifice of our lives just like Jesus Christ gave us His, then and only then will we begin to see how simple and uncomplicated the Lord really is. Sounds like a contradiction in terms to say the Lord is complicated yet simple at the same time but God is who He is yet is able to do what He does and only requires love and complete trust from us. The Lord will set up the time, place, and circumstances but you will have to set your mind and your will to go along with His plan.

I am not sure if this is the end of the story but for the sake of sharing the experience, it had to be told.

The End

Obedience Is Better

Obedience means to be submissive to the restraint or command of authority. The rules are the commandments the Lord has set for us to live by. Now what is the real meaning for obedience or obey? It is to comply with, be submissive to the restraint or command. Being obedient is not easy for those of us who can't seem to relinquish total control because that would be an act of blind faith.

I Sam 15:22 And Samuel said, Hath the LORD [as great] delight in burnt offerings and sacrifices, as in obeying the voice of the LORD? Behold, to obey [is] better than sacrifice, [and] to hearken than the fat of rams.

Yes, obedience is better.

But sometimes we think we can handle this little detail or manage that little state of affairs. If you are one of those people who have been able to solve your problem all on your own, please tell me how you did it. I have to be honest with you and admit that some time it is difficult to let the Lord handle every situation without trying to put my hands on. This is a personal thing that has to end up putting absolute trust and confident in God's ability to be God. He is who He is, the God of all creation of which we are, His creation.

Case in point, in the year of 2005 a pivotal moment happened in my life when the Lord told me to do something, which meant a gigantic leap of faith and unwavering trust in Him. It reminded me of when He told Abram to move to a place unknown to him. To pack his house to move, pack as if someone else were going to live there. I was to do the same thing and since my desire was to move anyway, I started collecting boxes and began packing, yet it still did not sound quite right. While in the garden God told Adam, what was required of him the dos and don'ts. Like Adam, my desire was to be obedient to the Lord as well, but I allowed the enemy to put just the smallest amount of doubt into my spirit as to what I was hearing. On occasion, we have the propensity to allow the majority to influence us to believe God does not work like that in this day and time even when the majority is one or two persons. The scripture that comes to my mind is *Matt 18:19 Again I say unto you, that if two of you shall agree on earth as touching anything that they shall ask, it shall be done for them of my Father which is in heaven.* In my mind, I thought I needed someone to touch and agree with what I had to do. Only thing is, I was the one who heard the instructions and only I could fulfill the task. This had to be my decision to be obedient because it had to be my choice to make.

Obedience is better.

We should always dare to be different and carry out those things that others will never accomplish to gain those things others will never obtain. *Act 22:14 and he said, The God of our fathers hath chosen thee, that thou shouldest know his will, and see that Just One, and shouldest hear the voice of his mouth.* Obedience will lead you down a path not well traveled by most and you will see few along the way. *Matt 22:14 say, "For many are called but few {are} chosen."* Just like the Lord Jesus was obedient and chose to do His Father 's will, we should do the same seeing we are joint heirs with Him.

It is better to be obedient.

When Israel decided they wanted to be like the nations around them and have a king, God told Samuel to let them know what treatment they should expect to receive and it would not be pleasant. They would again be servants, have their land taken, the young men would serve in the military and their daughters as domestic help. This story involved two separate incidents of disobedience, first there is the people and then Saul. It is curious how the act of not adhering to the word of God can foster a trend that can become common practice. Israel still wanted a human king so Samuel although he was not pleased with the decision put their petition before the Lord and He allowed it. Although it was not the time for this to happen, Samuel appointed Saul as king over an unprepared and impatient nation. Through one minuscule act of disobedience in his decision to not destroy all of the Amalekites and make their king a sacrificial offering to God, Saul made the error of a lifetime. The real sacrifice was the surrendering of his will to the will of God, which is always the acceptable action for all of us. But Saul thought this the honorable thing to do and he believed this would please the Lord and the people as well because he said to Samuel, I have performed the commandment of the LORD. How Saul must have felt to find out that his misjudgment or misinterpretation was an offence to the Lord, which had him removed as king. We are not responsible for what others do but we are responsible for doing what the Lord commands of us. Saul tried to blame the people but ultimately this was his directive to obey. *James 2:10 for whosoever shall keep the whole law, and yet offend in one point, he is guilty of all.*

Obedience is better.

One more scenario: Jonah also did his best not to obey the word of the Lord which was to go to Nineveh and tell the city that their wickedness had come up before the Lord and they were to be destroyed. Another struggle in our obedience is to lean to our own understanding and not as we are told. Jonah didn't like these people and felt they were getting a well-deserved punishment. If possible he would just avoid the whole matter and go a different way but it was not that simple. We always suffer for our stubbornness and sometimes others innocently suffer as well. He decided to take a sea journey in the opposite direction The storm that arose was different and the men on the ship to Tashish knew someone on it was out of order with the Lord. They had to find the one who was willing to risk their lives and rectify it the only way they knew how by the casting of lots.

Obedience is better than sacrifice.

When the lot fell on Jonah, they threw him overboard but the

Lord would not let it be that easy. No, he did not drown but into the belly of the fish prepared especially for him did he spend three days and nights. There in the darkness alone with his thoughts he had time to contemplate the error of his ways. When he decided it was better to obey, the fish spit him out on shore and he found it was not such a grievous task to accomplish and a whole city repented of the evil they had done and the Lord spared them.

What is better?

The bible compares rebellion to the sin of witchcraft, and stubbornness is as iniquity and idolatry. This is deep, but every time we fail to heed instruction to proceed in or refrain from an action or task assigned for our betterment, we could be committing an immoral sin. Ananias and his wife Sapphira chose to hold back a portion of the profit from selling their property and because their deceitfulness was the sin of omission they suffered a quick punishment right on the spot - they died. I believe since God's wrath is not always swift but merciful toward us as stated in *Ephesians 2:4 But God, who is rich in mercy, for his great love wherewith he loved us,* we appear to have escaped. Is disobedience ever worth it?

To get back to my story I must say along with obedience comes patience because sometimes we don't see the results of our assignment revealed immediately. Therefore, I continued to pack expecting to move at any time. Although there will always be a doubting Thomas in the crowd who will only believe if they can put their hand in it, it was my obedience that was in question. I had to trust the task given to me was from the Lord. The results came one year later, when I moved to Chicago and someone else is now living in my house. A minor choice to be subservient led to a mammoth leap of faith. Doors were opened, opportunities were presenting themselves, and I had been situated or positioned to move to another realm with a new attitude of what obedience to God could do. If there were any lessons to learn, it would be to relinquish total control and to be submissive in all areas of life because to obey will always gives you nothing to lose and everything to gain. I will leave you with this scripture of who and whose you are in order to aid in the building of your faith and encourage you to keep this in mind. *Romans 6:16 Know ye not, that to whom ye yield yourselves servants to obey, his servants ye are to whom ye obey; whether of sin unto death, or of obedience unto righteousness?*

Better to obey.

CONTEMPLATIVE MOMENTS

1. What is your definition of obedience?

2. Did you have a Jonah experience?

3. What were your results?

Times Three

U sually you lay down, have a dream that you may or may not remember or you might not dream at all. This is not the case for me. I am what you may call a vivid dreamer, full of color, crazy events and telling stories. This dream was instructional and very meaningful for my life and the things I have to do to fulfill my purpose.

We all have purpose which is either done according to plan or done the way we think it should be. My purpose has to be done according to the plan set before me but sometime the lines of communication are a little blurred by the cloud of life's experiences. Well, this dream was just another way of letting me have a little glimpse into a much clearer vision of what is expected of me and what I have to do.

It started with what appeared to be a large wagon wheel spinning around in front of me. There were upside down words on the wheel with spaces between them. The wheel was spinning for what felt like a long time and then it stopped. I still couldn't make out the words but then a voice said "you have to fill in the blanks." At that point I woke up and contemplated what weird thing had just happened. This was not my first strange dream and surely not my last because when I when back to sleep, guess what. There I was standing in front of that wheel for a second time watching it spin around again with the unreadable words. The wheel stopped and I heard the same voice say once again "you have to fill in the blanks."

I knew this had to mean something important for me, because I have never had the exact same dream in one night, really never had the same dream. This time I got up for a drink of water and wondered if I would ever get the interpretation for it. Okay, it was the middle of the night so I went back to bed, guess what. For the third time I was back in the dream in front of the wheel. The wheel stopped for the third time and the voice said "you have to fill in the blanks." After that dream I was up for the rest of the night.

So what could all that possibly mean, a wheel turning, a voice saying, and words with spaces to be filled. This is an interpretation I received: Dreamer, Because of the reoccurrence of this 3 times it seems you are having difficulty seeing the completeness of the word of God and there is something you must do to adjust this. These dreams come for you to see this more clearly, confront it, and seek God for His wisdom, understanding and help in receiving greater clarity into His word. Because of this, I not only read more to gain knowledge I need in my writing but I study the word for His approval in my life. Blessings have come on my journey with the Lord.

CONTEMPLATIVE MOMENTS

Journal your dreams

Who's in the Box?

The Lord is in certainty true to His Word. It is His spoken word and I believe it. He once told me that I would see visions but I had my own preconceived notions of how that would happen. The Lord said His ways are far beyond ours and we can't even imagine what His thoughts are like. In my mind's eye, the visions would be of future events of great magnitude and wondrous sights, sometimes good and sometimes bad. They would seem so realistic that I would feel like I was right there almost a participant. Well, I am not seeing things quite that way.

We always say that we limit God when we are actually the ones who have not released ourselves to the limitless, matchless God that He is. While contemplating this I saw a vision of a small clear box and in the box, there existed a whole world with a beautiful sky, sun, moon, stars trees, birds, and people - it was a real place. It was our world, as we know it with all its restrictions. It was set in the middle of another world in which I saw no limits. The same elements existed in that bigger world like in the smaller version but everything was so much more brilliant and more defined.

In the miniature box, I could see people going about their

everyday lives, praying, worshipping and have faith in God to a certain point. But when the time comes to believe and trust Him for what He told us would be, we have a tendency to hold back and hold back big time. We act as though it's too much to trust Him beyond what we can see or imagine. Our belief is to the sky because we say it is the limit (in the box). It's not a bad thing but there is always more to achieve.

When Abram obeyed the Lords' leading and left from amongst his people, he took his nephew Lot with him. The scripture does not state if this was what the Lord had in mind but sometime we embellish on the word given to us. The reason I question Abram's decision to bring family that he could have left them behind avoiding unnecessary strife.

However, what if we would peradventure and lift one flap on that self-made box to let God's potential shine in. Our vision has just increased by twenty five percent. We can now see what He has for us in the north. It could be a better understanding of His word, how it works in the area of healing. *Isaiah 53:5 but he was wounded for our transgressions,he was bruised for our iniquities: the chastisement of our peace was upon him; and with his stripes we are healed.* Moreover, because of this we are beginning to believe that Jesus will heal all our diseases and mind hang-ups. We trust Him just that much more as we begin to transform into climbers.

With a newfound strength, we are able to lift the second flap in the south and with an unquestioning action such as that, we have a fresh respect of Jesus and how much He loves us. The love is so great that He lets us share in His relationship with His Father. We have the privilege of being joint heirs and now we will have even more knowledge of our authority over every trick of the enemy <u>fifty percent</u> closer.

By now, we have gained a little more power over doubt so we can lift a third flap out of the way in the east. By this time a head, both arms and your upper torso will be teetering over the edge of your box. The view has changed from the ordinary to the extraordinary. You are wishing someone else were making their way out of their self-imposed limitations into the realm of Godly expectations. You are <u>seventy five percent</u> absolutely trusting in Jesus.

After having our eyes opened to how much we set boundaries on ourselves, revelation has cross the threshold of our very being that spiritually and naturally so all things are in actual fact possible. We now have total trust in the Creator for what we ask for, desire and need. In the west, the last flap lifted and we are free to experience God's glory. We are now on the threshold of seeing the reality of what this world is really all about and letting the Lord be the extreme Deity He already is.

We are <u>hundred percent</u> in a boundless realm and the lights are brighter, the sounds are sharper and air is fresher our visions are His which makes His vision ours and suddenly we see that all things are justifiably possible. Now we are free and let loose into the four corners of world, the heavens and God's limitations of which there are none because we have the authority of our Big Brother, Jesus Christ which gives us entitlement to all God has planned for us.

Abram gave Lot first choice of where he wanted to live but then he questioned if he had allowed him to pick the better territory. *Gen 13:11 Then Lot chose him all the plain of Jordan; and Lot journeyed east: and they separated themselves the one from the other.* Abram was limited to what he thought he saw and that was only a little portion of what God had for him but when he allowed his faith to lift him out of the box from the place he was, he saw a magnificent view. Scripture says *in Gen 13: 14 And the LORD said unto Abram, after that Lot was separated from him, Lift up now thine eyes, and look from the place where thou art northward, and southward, and eastward, and westward: 15 For all the land which thou seest, to thee will I give it, and to thy seed forever.* I can imagine you see our vision is better out of the box, too. Abram looking in every direction and saying, I did not see all this the first time but with second sight, I must worship the Lord with His promises now fulfilled and those to come.

My advice is get out, get out and again I say get out of that limiting, not enough room for growth, stifling box where you have allowed life and people to determine how much potential you have. Let the Nay Sayers have their point of view as narrow minded as it may be but as for all who are willing to take the challenge, it is well worth the climb.

Oh, the endless possibilities - all is possible.

CONTEMPLATIVE MOMENTS

1. Share some thoughts about how you see things

2. What would you like to see?

3. Share or explain your box experience

Misery Loves Misery

I realize that misery doesn't really need company because when it is set in your spirit, it is content to entertain itself. It will rationalizes the pain it feels as normal, the loneliness as part of its personality, and the frustration of not getting what it wants as someone else's fault. When looking up the word *content,* I found many synonyms for it such as pleased, satisfied, contented, comfortable, calm, just to mention a few. The word *misery* means unhappiness, melancholy, depression, sorrow, sadness. When you put it all together misery is pleased in unhappiness, satisfied to be melancholy, contented with depression, comfortable at sorrow, and calm amidst sadness.

At the times of feeling sorry for yourself, notice how many times "*I*" fills your mind. I can't do this or I don't have that, I feel left out this situation, or I am always blamed for that. Imagine having a party and only needing to send out one invitation but then why send out any when you will be the only on the list anyway. Misery does not need any fanfare, any marching band, or colored balloons because it is its own self-contained, self-revealing, self-edifying entity.

Complaints can be all defeating but the Lord has a plan for our good and He intents for us to have the best He has to offer. The enemy of our life and our future wants us to focus on the minuscule things that are neither important nor long lasting. For some the miseries of life have become the norm, commonplace or what they are accustomed to. But what if we focus on the positive things that are promised to keep our minds and heart at peace. Purposefully counting our blessings until they gloriously overtake us as the Father intended. *2 Corinthians 1:3-4 (3) Blessed {be} God, even the Father of our Lord Jesus Christ, the Father of mercies, and the God of all comfort; (4) Who comforteth us in all our tribulation, that we may be able to comfort them which are in any trouble, by the comfort wherewith we ourselves are comforted of God.* Look at that, the Lord wants to comfort us so why not let Him.

Misery needs to be its own companion and not yours but with all the complaining, discontent and downright disrespect we show our Father by our insistence on being unhappy, it's like another slap in the face to our Lord and it hurts. Is life ever as bad as we let on? No, it's not. It can be a mind over matter situation if our mind is concentrated on the right matter and if we let this mind be in us that is in Christ Jesus the matter is in His hand anyway. When we replay our problems over again, we animate them to do just what we say because there is power in the tongue. I heard a message that reinforced the fact that we have strength enough to be happy. There is a popular song that tells us, don't worry - be happy. The word of God put the ultimate topper on happiness when it says in *Ps 144:15 Happy is that people, that is in such a case: yea, happy is that people, whose God is the LORD.* In this psalm, the writer is referring to the mercies and blessings of God, how increases come to those who put their trust in Him. How happy is that?

Maybe if we didn't reside in the problems of this life, we could actually see the joy we have even when things don't seem to go our way because they really are for our good. *Rom 5: 2 by whom also we have access by faith into this grace wherein we stand, and rejoice in hope of the glory of God.* If we can learn the lesson that comes around so often to not allow misery to make us make ourselves miserable, then we can learn that the power of happiness is already inside us. We can do all things through God when we use the strength He lovingly provides. So let's make it so, so we can trust that whatever the situation, it is as temporary as temporary can be whether it is sickness, loneliness, shortage of funds, or so many other things - it won't last forever.

Smile and be of good cheer and let it be contagious in a good way proving our Father is able to be the one bright spot in our lives that makes it all worthwhile. How simple is that?

CONTEMPLATIVE MOMENTS

1. Describe your miserable moment

2. What has helped you through it?

3. What advice would you give to help someone else?

Process It

With the dawning of each day, I am learning more and more about the process. It is the process of time and the waiting period. It is learning the process of struggle and the release of it, the process of forgiveness, and the giving of it. There are so many processes used to accomplish and achieve an anticipated conclusion.

On my job, I learned the different aspects involved in the performance of it and it was challenging to say the least. Every week a new element was added revealing each intricate piece and how it panned out in the whole scheme of it. It would be great if the whole process was laid out before me with each little part explained in detail with nothing missing. It is a credit to the teacher or mentor when the lessons are not held back to avoid errors.

It doesn't always work out that way and neither does the processes in life. There are instructions given which gives you the first step with several procedures to them. Step 1 may have an A B C and each one needs completion before starting the next step. It seems I am always writing in some form or fashion about how multi-faceted life is; simple as it is complicated. The roadblocks are many some time hard to avoid but tenuous trying to get through. The process is an abstract course to say the least with many hurdles to overcome.

The bible says the race is not given to the swift or even the strong but to the one that stays the course. Stay within the process.

Between a Rock
and a Hard Place

You know how it feels to be between a rock and a hard place. It's difficult because you often don't know which way to turn nor do you have enough room to move. Maybe life has backed you into a corner with no way out. No matter what solution you come up with, it is never enough to solve the problem. Plan A didn't work, Plan B was not sufficient and by the time you got to Plan C, you had to clean up the mess from the other two plans. That rock and that hard place can be a miserable place (but the Rock). Most of the time we use that phrase with a negative nuance but only because the things we go through don't always feel good. Think about your last hard place experience and you will find that something unexpectedly good came out of it. It may have been a sad place (JOY FILLER), a lonely place (PATIENCE GIVER), a trying place (ENDURANCE MAKER), whatever may come next place (STEP ORDERER) or I can't go any further place (STRENGTH BUILDER).

These are some examples of a rock place we may experience but guess what; the Lord is the Rock of ages for anything and everything. He told Peter that upon this rock, I will build my church and the gates of hell shall not prevail against it. If that is not a solid foundation, I do not know what is. *Deuteronomy 32:4 says He is the Rock, his work is perfect, a God of truth.* It can be a good place.

When God wanted to communicate with Moses and Moses needed to talk to God, He put him in a rock place. Moses was positioned by God on a hard place in a cleft of the rock and covered by God's hand. Because of this positioning, Moses was able to have the desire of his heart and that was to see God's Glory. He had the courage to face a rebellious people with the word written by the finger of the Almighty God. That was his rock and a hard place. Mortal man could not see the Lord's full glory and live, so the Father shielded Moses for his own protection but he saw what he needed to see. He was able to receive instruction and have an intimate encounter experiencing God's presence. *Songs of Solomon 2:14 places you in the cleft of the rock, in the secret places of the stairs and He want to hear your sweet voice.*

It's beautiful the intimate times the Lord wants to share with us. He knows those rough times, those frustrating situations and even those devastating moments, yet we can land on the rock for security and comfort.

Daniel was another one caught between two opinions. In his case, he could either obey the decree not to worship any god for thirty days or obey his Lord in whom he had full trust. He decided to obey the Lord and do what was his normal routine, which was to pray in full sight with the windows open. What nerve he had. Into the lion's den he went. The rock was the pit and the lion's mouth, a hard place. Nevertheless, even there, I could hear him sending up fervent prayers powerful enough to shut the lion's mouth tight. Even in the face of danger, the Lord's name is a strong tower where we can find safety.

Then, what happened with Job - can anyone tell me? He was doing all he could to serve the Lord. God even testified about him to the enemy. It just goes to show that you can live a righteous life, having all your oars in the water and life still rocks the boat knocking you clean out of it In one day Job lost everything he had which included family, livelihood, and substance. His rock was his faithfulness to God and his hard place was the testing of that faith. God knows who we are, what we are capable of, and what we will do but some time we have to see it. The road is not always easy but only the way of a transgressor is hard. Scripture says that we have light afflictions because His yolk is easy and His burdens are light. That rock and that hard place is merely a trying of our faith.

I can go on and on with stories from the bible where the Lord has shown Himself to be protection and a solid foundation but here is one of my own rock and a hard place experiences. My story may not be as unusual as when Moses faced the Red Sea or Daniel's lockjaw lion encounter but it is my testimony.

You probably expect me to have some elaborate tale of great proportions but for me, my rock and my hard place came late in 1977. I was watching a popular religious program and although nothing special was said, it made me realized that if the Lord had decided to call me home; I would not have liked the living arrangements. You see I was one of those transgressors on my way to hell the hard way. The hard way you may ask, the answer is yes the hard way. Here it is plain and simple, I thought I was doing all right in my sins but did not consider that if I wasn't living for God, my master was the devil. No way can we serve two masters without loving one and hating the other. In my mind, I was a good Christian despite the fact that it was in name only and my life was not glorifying the Lord.

Watching that program was a turning point in my life because it made me see the sad state of my situation. I didn't drink, smoke, nor did I commit any of what we consider major sins if there is such a thing but I was lost just the same. Being a good person was just not enough to make it into heaven and living a lukewarm existence was all I needed to do to ensure in my place in hell. I had to make the decision of my life and it was a choice between having a rock fall on me and landing permanently in a hard place or standing on the Rock. I decided to go with the Rock of my salvation, the Rock that is higher than I am. The Rock of ages, Jesus is His name. He has been my solid foundation and all that life is. *Proverbs 18:10 says the name of the LORD is a strong tower: the righteous runneth into it, and is safe.* That was a great beginning and the best decision I have ever made. Please make Him your rock and He will rock your world forever.

CONTEMPLATIVE MOMENT

1. How did you manage the hard place in your life?

2. When did you realize Jesus Christ was your rock?

3. How did you feel when the Lord delivered you?

Idle – Mind and Body and Spirit

I have noticed something about myself and that is when I let my mind wander randomly, not very productive. The ideas are not always the best and are usually concerning things I can't change nor should I want to. However, if I put my mind to the tasks ahead that can and will produce more fruitful and creative endeavors there is always a better result.

The statement often used about an idle mind being the devil's workshop is not biblical nor is it a real quote. But it is based on truths that say idleness is not what a Christian or child of God should ever be found doing. *Proverb 13:27* states that a good wife looks out for her household and is always busy doing what needs to be done and does it well. There should never be a time when we say there is nothing to do because prayer is always appropriate and will keep your mind busy focusing on the things of the Lord. So prayer is something to help the mind but there are other ways we are idle and that is in deeds.

If we all would think about how lazy we are in doing work for the Lord that much can be missed by our procrastination. One of my biggest hindrances is letting things go until the last minute and on occasion just being too late. I can't tell you how many times I just let the deadline go by henceforth missing out on benefits I could have use or adventures I could have enjoyed. Lazy that's all, just plain lazy but who did I cause to miss out on their blessing. Now I'm not going to take all the blame because we all have been guilty of idleness in one form or another. *Proverbs 19:15* talk about our slothfulness that causes us to go into a deep sleep and an idle soul makes us hungry. That is interpreted to say idleness can cause us to sleep the day away getting nothing accomplished and if you don't work you can't eat. The hungry could also represent the soul being denied the nourishment to help it to grow stronger. Oh taste and see that the Lord, He is good and what we do will go up to the glory and honor of the Lord like a sweet smelling savor to His nostrils as well. *That's a little food for thought.*

During my preparation for retirement, I actually started thinking of a life outside of the work I routinely performed for many years which meant having to establish another routine or maybe no routine at all for the rest of my life, the latter sounds best. However I am one who likes to stay active so I had think of options to accomplish but at a slower pace. Although there may not be an alarm clock to answer, I will still have to answer to something or someone.

That reminds me of a story in *Matthew 6* telling about a man who was looking out over his field and saw work to be done but he needed laborers. So he went to the marketplace about the third hour and saw many standing idle and offered them work for a set wage. Again he went to the marketplace at a later hour and saw still more standing idle so he gave them the same deal as the others. Yet again at the end of the day at the same place there were others not doing anything. As you can see at any hour of the day the master of the field found idle people. Just because they didn't have employment, they could have been useful in some capacity. The story goes on to say the master rewarded the late comers at the same rate as those that began earlier. No matter what age, physical ability, or financial status there is some purpose for all of us, so please don't say there is nothing to do. The harvest is plentiful but the willing laborers are few. We should always be busy, not just running in place or all over the place busy but with a purposeful goal leading to an expected end which is the plan set for us before our time began. To say again that an idle mind is the devil's workshop, I think not because an idle mind is really not working. Remember the topic is still idleness.

Thought I was finished so you can see how quickly the mind can become nonfunctioning right in the midst of very productive work. Let me clarify this statement, daydreaming or fantasizing is not always a bad thing especially when it's about tangible, attainable ideas concerning short or long-term goals. We need to picture in our mind's eye how to work out the details of that which has not happened yet. It sounds like the faith imaginary the bible speaks of when it says faith without works is dead or we walk by faith not by sight. So watch not to speak idle words that are not in God's plan because in the tongue exists life or death and we can prophesy either one. If you want it let your mind see it, let your words speak it then let your actions live it and have it.

The one thing I want leave with you is, occupy your mind with larger than life hopes and dreams and expect greater than you can ever hope or dream for, that is a good use of the mind.

Idle Definitions

Frivolous and a waste of time

Unlikely to be carried out or impossible to put into effect

Not working, operating, producing, or in use

The state in which a motor vehicle engine is running but not in gear

Pass time aimlessly – idled the time away

Futile – in vain

Pointless – without purpose or benefit

Worthless – having no value

Speculative – theoretical, not practical

Ineffectual – insufficient to produce a desired effect

CONTEMPLATIVE MOMENTS

.

The ramblings of a productive mind

Truth Be Told

If the truth were told, you would not hear it from the adversary. If he can get you to believe a half-truth; a whole lie will be coming soon. This is a sad scenario but so many people have chosen to believe partial truths because it fits their lifestyle and is acceptable enough to allow having one foot in the church and one foot in the world. My former pastor always taught the congregation never to accept everything that was said from the pulpit without reading or searching it out for yourself.

It's an embarrassment to know that many of us are willing to accept a man's opinions and/or interpretations as the gospel when it has no scriptural basis. If the enemy can make us believe a lie, he will and any way he can deceive; he would even lie to the very elect. It is time to decide whom will we serve. If God is God, then serve Him and if Baal were god then serve him. *Psalm 33:4 for the word of the LORD is right; and all his works are done in truth.*

Before going too deep into the word, I would like to skim across the surface of how the enemy tries to deceive us with half-truths. Some of us are the called and chosen to some extraordinary work for the Lord. We are exceptionally gifted, anointed and equipped to accomplish the tasks that have been set before us and because we are such a threat we are hinder at every turn *1Peter 5:8 be sober, be vigilant; because your adversary the devil, as a roaring lion, walketh about, seeking whom he may devour.*

I am reminded of the first lie told to the first, first lady in the bible and that was to none other than Miss Eve herself. There she was minding her own business, having not long been presented to Adam as a companion, helpmeet, and wife and with Adam, she was enjoying what God lovingly provided for her. If I may set the scene for the trick of the enemy, it started with the Father's instruction to Adam on his purpose of being placed in the garden. His assignment was to have dominion over the earth and the creatures on earth and the foul of the air and the fish in the sea.

SIDEBAR: We were made in His image so He must have held us in high regard making us a little lower than the angels in heaven and allowing us to have full fellowship with Him at all times. I must continue with the story. The Lord Father told Adam which trees were good for eating but one tree that was forbidden fruit and the scripture reads like this: *Genesis 2:15-17 15. And the LORD God took the man, and put him into the Garden of Eden to dress it and to keep it. 16. And the LORD God commanded the man, saying, of every tree of the garden thou mayest freely eat: 17. But of the tree of the knowledge of good and evil, thou shalt not eat of it: for in the day that thou eatest thereof thou shalt surely die.* This deserves repeating, *and the LORD God commanded the man* not the woman what should not to be eaten.

ANOTHER SIDEBAR: Since a day with the Lord is like a thousand years and a thousand years is one day, were the six days of creation of this world accomplished in a twenty-four-hour span each or in eternity which is timeless? This is interesting because we know that God's time is not our time with His ways being far above ours. Imagine the thought He used in making the earth green the mountains brown and red and gray with the sky and the oceans a matching blue that when you look out upon the horizon you can't tell where one ends and the other begins, well His thoughts are even greater than that. Read *II Peter 3:7-9 for* more on the time factor but now back to the story at hand. It seems like both Adam and Eve were around for a while and so I am sure at some point in time he informed her of what the Lord commanded of him to do. With the man being the head of the woman and not wanted her to be totally ignorant of what the Lord required; I am sure Adam informed her of this truth.

Don't think Satan wasn't lurking somewhere in the shadows just waiting for his opportunity to wreak havoc with God's plan and sway man/woman from his/her purpose. *Proverbs 12:17 "He that speaketh truth sheweth forth righteousness: but a false witness deceit"* and that is Satan in a nutshell, a false witness. Eve may have been more vulnerable in the sense that she may not have been as aware that the word given by God was the truth because she had not established a relationship with God like Adam. Please understand that I am using creative license here when I talk about Eve's relationship with the Lord because the bible does not say much about her God walk but I am not excusing her actions. Eve could have used this opportunity to seek the Lord for her direction. *Psalm 86:11 Teach me thy way, O LORD; I will walk in thy truth: unite my heart to fear thy name.*

SIDEBAR FOR A THIRD TIME: It is our responsibility to try the spirit by the spirit *1 John 4:1 Beloved, believe not every spirit, but try the spirits whether they are of God: because many false prophets are gone out into the world.* There is truth, and there is a real truth and we have a responsibility to make sure what we hear, is the absolute and unconditional word of God spoken from His lips to your ear. You are worth the wait as God prepares you for the mate of your destiny, you can strive for that promotion because of your favor with the King, and you are rich beyond measure because your Father owns the universe. His word is truth. Let us continue.

Why would Eve believe the half-truth of a serpent, a snake, a nonhuman, and not the word of the Lord? My conclusion is that it sounded reasonable that they wouldn't surely die. A God who had shown them such love and consideration would not let the relationship end like that. Sometimes sin can sound like a reasonable solution to the quandary we often find ourselves in when we choose to disobey or maybe just not fully trust the true word of God.

The enemy knows the truth because of the relationship he had with the real Word but he deceived his own self when he believed his own hype. The result was being kick out of heaven. A quote from Sir Walter Scott comes to mind and it goes like this; "Oh What a tangled web we weave when first we practice to deceive". If you have ever walked into a spider web, you know how it can wrap all around you getting all in your hair, on your face and on your clothes. The more you twist or turn to break free, the more you are entwined It attaches itself to you and makes it difficult to remove all the sticky residue that have been left behind, that is the same effect those half-truths have on our lives. The residue is the hurt, distrust, guilt, and the un-forgiveness left for the deceived to attempt to get rid of. The pattern woven is not pretty nor is it advantageous to the fulfilling of your purpose but it is to ensnare the children of God into believing a lie. God cannot lie nor will He deceive.

Satan as the serpent convinced Eve into believing some of the truth and enticed them both into disobeying God's commandment and all three suffered for their part in the subterfuge. Because of their error humanity suffered as well. Our fate now is the same as Adam and Eve to work by the sweat of our brow and bare pain in childbirth. But we also lost that childlike innocence by knowing evil exists which instilled a longing for the fine and simple life God created us to enjoy. The truth being told it could have been all good.

SIDEBAR FOUR: *3John 11 Beloved, follow not that which is evil, but that which is good. He that doeth good is of God: but he that doeth evil hath not seen God.* Truth is the real state of things, fact, honesty and a true or accepted statement or proposition. The problem we seem to have with the truth is that it does not allow us the freedom to do whatever we please and seemingly get away with it. The Lord said He was going to prepare a place for us and if it were not so He would not have told us. He said that our latter would be better, no he said greater than our former and it is a true statement because He is not a man that He would lie to us. What would God have to gain by not being forthright with us being He has it all is all and created it all. Now Satan on the other hand had it all then lost it all by wanting the absolute all that all belonged to God. Sorry I cannot seem to help adding my creative touches

Let us read His word to know the truth, believe His word to have the truth, wrap you in His word to live the truth, and then trust His word to be the truth. If the truth were told, it is, has always been and will always be the unadulterated word of God and the word is His Son, Jesus Christ. Trust Him.

SIDEBAR to explain the SIDEBARS: I hope that you are not too confused with all the sidebars. The sidebars are thoughts brought on by either a word or a phrase from the story above that stirred my imagination and made me think of the little details we may miss while only looking at the big picture. Now, please don't make me explain the explanation.

CONTEMPLATIVE MOMENTS

NOTES:

Perceptions

I think therefore I am." I must find out who made that statement so I can give them the credit for it. However, it's so true that we are what we think but most of us become less than what we can be. The way we see things will help to shape our lives ergo, good perceptions are important for bringing out the best in us. We can live in a ghetto but not be ghetto minded or we can have all the best life has to offer but still not have class. Sometimes we put up a facade or an illusion of happiness when in reality, we are screaming for help but no one hears us because of the screams in their own ears. Most of this is an elevated ego or low self-esteem issue with the ego thinking more highly than it should and low self-esteem wondering what others may think. Granted, this statement may only be true for this story but again it is only my perception.

What might we look like from the inside out? Are you a beautiful person physically but with an ugly heart? What would you do if you could see that person that lurks on the inside? Please don't think this is a put down because I realize that our perception of ourselves was formed early in life, as children. Many people may have already dealt with the negative words and moved on to form their own ideas of who they are with positive results. Then there are the others like me who still have a difficult time moving past the past. There must be a release of messed up thoughts and ideas of who really lives on the inside crying, scratching and digging to get out. There must be discernment in the body of Christ.

Try this: to see what you think of yourself, stand in front of a mirror without makeup, uncombed hair, or brushed teeth. With the real you looking back, let the discussion begin. There you are without any pretense or illusion of beauty, which help to make us feel good about ourselves. You are face to face with the real you with all flaws visible looking you in the face. I hope that the image staring back at you is a good one and no matter what others may see, you see all the beauty the Lord intended you to see. This is because God doesn't make junk.

The exercise above is a physical one, but we also should look at the person within and this requires another viewpoint reconfiguration. Your self-worth is also in the mirror of your mind that is not as easy to deal with. The perception we have of our inner self is a powerful image that should always be positive and should help to shape our character and the way we treat ourselves and others. Therefore, I would advise you not to tell your children they are bad when they are only learning the boundary and limitation of social behavior. This is not an attempt to analyze neither a claim to be an expert in social behavior but I am an expert at being a child who had many unconstructive comments communicated to her. The question is, am I willing to share any of this with all of you and expose myself once more to scrutiny? Yes, I will be obedient for the sake of the call on my life.

Let me share an experience of how you may see yourself when you have digested a negative image diet from a young age. Some time ago, I went to Youngstown to visit my cousin Pam. We talked and enjoyed our visit catching up on the time we missed together. Eventually the family album was brought out for a flash back into both of our lives. While looking over my life and the people that affected it, I saw a particular picture of my late brother Jerry, his wife Janet (also deceased), my late husband Leon, and this beautiful young woman who I could not identify. Now, someone had once told me that I was the runt of the bunch, not that attractive, and a whole shade darker than the rest of the family. After seeing that picture with Leon in it, I knew that I had be there too. Therefore, I asked what sounded like a dumb question but I just needed to know the answer. The question was about the identity of the girl in the picture. After giving me a puzzled look she said the girl was me. In my mind, I thought it could have been me but I never saw myself as beautiful because my perception was warped.

Could someone please tell me why we attempt to make ourselves feel better by making others feel small, insecure thus holding someone back from life's wonderful potential? There are many times I've heard the phase "Just get over it" and trust me I am still trying to get rid of the residue of it. Many of you may be in the same situation, trying to get over it. I know that beauty is only surface deep but the beauty coming from within enables us to love those who tried to hinder or impede the high self-esteem we should hold for ourselves knowing we are children of the King.

With knowledge of whose I am, the battle for confidence is already won. I only have to cross the finish line for I have already defeated the enemy who attempted to steal my self-confidence big time. Moreover, if I can do it we all can.

My last comment is: Stop the abuse on the young lives entrusted to your care by always encouraging them to be all they can be and know that all things are possible through Jesus Christ our Lord even if you can't see it, still anything is possible. Look how well you turned out.

The famous French philosopher and mathematician René Descartes, also known as the Father of Modern Philosophy is responsible for the opening statement of this story.

CONTEMPLATIVE MOMENTS

1. How do you see yourself?

2. What did the mirror experience show you?

3. What is your definition of beauty?

ABOUT THE AUTHOR

Gwendolyn Jackson is the co-founder of Abundant Harvest COGIC in Buffalo. NY. She has held several positions there including Sunday School Superintendent, President of the Women's Department, and Trustee. She was Assistant District Missionary and president of the Christian Women Council in Chicago, Il. Currently she Is president of NCOURAGEME2BUNLIMITED a nonprofit organization. To her credit she has produced a play and the original songs performed in it. She is the proud mother of six children, twenty-three grandchildren and one great grandson. Buffalo, NY is where she calls home.

www.ingramcontent.com/pod-product-compliance
Lightning Source LLC
LaVergne TN
LVHW022318080426
835509LV00036B/2590